GREAT EXIT PROJECTS ON THE
US
CONSTITUTION

GREAT SOCIAL STUDIES EXIT PROJECTS™

GREAT EXIT PROJECTS ON THE
US
CONSTITUTION

Bridey Heing

rosen publishing's
rosen
central®

New York

Published in 2020 by The Rosen Publishing Group, Inc.
29 East 21st Street, New York, NY 10010

Copyright © 2020 by The Rosen Publishing Group, Inc.

First Edition

Library of Congress Cataloging-in-Publication Data

Names: Heing, Bridey, author.
Title: Great exit projects on the US Constitution / Bridey Heing.
Description: New York : Rosen Publishing, 2020. | Series: Great social studies exit projects | Audience: Grades 5–8. | Includes bibliographical references and index.
Identifiers: LCCN 2018016610| ISBN 9781499440461 (library bound) | ISBN 9781499440454 (pbk.)
Subjects: LCSH: Constitutional law—United States—Juvenile literature. | Constitutional history—United States—Juvenile literature.
Classification: LCC KF4550 .H45 2018 | DDC 342.73—dc23
LC record available at https://lccn.loc.gov/2018016610

Manufactured in the United States of America

CONTENTS

6 **INTRODUCTION**

9 **CHAPTER ONE**
COLONIAL AMERICA

18 **CHAPTER TWO**
WRITING THE CONSTITUTION

26 **CHAPTER THREE**
A MORE PERFECT UNION

36 **CHAPTER FOUR**
THE LEGISLATIVE BRANCH

42 **CHAPTER FIVE**
THE EXECUTIVE BRANCH

49 **CHAPTER SIX**
THE JUDICIAL BRANCH

55 **GLOSSARY**
57 **FOR MORE INFORMATION**
60 **FOR FURTHER READING**
61 **BIBLIOGRAPHY**
62 **INDEX**

The US Constitution is an unrivaled feat in the history of nation building. Written in the aftermath of war, created by representatives of largely autonomous states with conflicting interests and concerns, and forged out of a compromise between two proposals that differed in spirit as well as design, the Constitution is widely recognized as the world's oldest constitution still being used today. At the time it was written, it was the first founding document of its kind, creating a whole new form of government. But in the centuries since it was ratified, it has become an inspiration for democratic states around the world.

Yet the Constitution is also controversial and has been from its earliest days. Tensions over states' rights were one of the driving forces in the blended system of federal and local governance that the Constitution enshrines, but those tensions were not resolved by the document. The Constitution was also designed to be flexible, introducing amendments as a way to alter the document as time went on and new issues emerged. But even so, today debates rage around the country about how the Constitution should be interpreted and when it should be amended, or if doing so too often will set a dangerous precedent.

In 1787, eleven years after the Declaration of Independence set out the hopes of a fledgling nation, some of the United States' greatest early leaders met in Philadelphia to create a new form of government. The Philadelphia Convention brought together fifty-five delegates from the newly formed United States, with all states represented except Rhode Island. The men representing their country spent months debating forms of government, modes of

We the People

of the United States, in order to form a more perfect Union, establish Justice, insure domestic Tranquility, provide for the common defence, promote the general Welfare, and secure the Blessings of Liberty to ourselves and our Posterity, do ordain and establish this Constitution for the United States of America.

Article. I.

Section. 1. All legislative Powers herein granted shall be vested in a Congress of the United States, which shall consist of a Senate and House of Representatives.

Section. 2. The House of Representatives shall be composed of Members chosen every second Year by the People of the several States, and the Electors in each State shall have the Qualifications requisite for Electors of the most numerous Branch of the State Legislature.

No Person shall be a Representative who shall not have attained to the Age of twenty five Years, and been seven Years a Citizen of the United States, and who shall not, when elected, be an Inhabitant of that State in which he shall be chosen.

Representatives and direct Taxes shall be apportioned among the several States which may be included within this Union, according to their respective Numbers, which shall be determined by adding to the whole Number of free Persons, including those bound to Service for a Term of Years, and excluding Indians not taxed, three fifths of all other Persons. The actual Enumeration shall be made within three Years after the first Meeting of the Congress of the United States, and within every subsequent Term of ten Years, in such Manner as they shall by Law direct. The Number of Representatives shall not exceed one for every thirty Thousand, but each State shall have at Least one Representative; and until such enumeration shall be made, the State of New Hampshire shall be entitled to chuse three, Massachusetts eight, Rhode Island and Providence Plantations one, Connecticut five, New York six, New Jersey four, Pennsylvania eight, Delaware one, Maryland six, Virginia ten, North Carolina five, South Carolina five, and Georgia three.

When vacancies happen in the Representation from any State, the Executive Authority thereof shall issue Writs of Election to fill such Vacancies.

The House of Representatives shall chuse their Speaker and other Officers; and shall have the sole Power of Impeachment.

Section. 3. The Senate of the United States shall be composed of two Senators from each State, chosen by the Legislature thereof, for six Years; and each Senator shall have one Vote.

Immediately after they shall be assembled in Consequence of the first Election, they shall be divided as equally as may be into three Classes. The Seats of the Senators of the first Class shall be vacated at the Expiration of the second Year, of the second Class at the Expiration of the fourth Year, and of the third Class at the Expiration of the sixth Year, so that one third may be chosen every second Year; and if Vacancies happen by Resignation, or otherwise, during the Recess of the Legislature of any State, the Executive thereof may make temporary Appointments until the next Meeting of the Legislature, which shall then fill such Vacancies.

No Person shall be a Senator who shall not have attained to the Age of thirty Years, and been nine Years a Citizen of the United States, and who shall not, when elected, be an Inhabitant of that State for which he shall be chosen.

The Vice President of the United States shall be President of the Senate, but shall have no Vote, unless they be equally divided.

The Senate shall chuse their other Officers, and also a President pro tempore, in the Absence of the Vice President, or when he shall exercise the Office of President of the United States.

The Senate shall have the sole Power to try all Impeachments. When sitting for that Purpose, they shall be on Oath or Affirmation. When the President of the United States is tried, the Chief Justice shall preside: And no Person shall be convicted without the Concurrence of two thirds of the Members present.

Judgment in Cases of Impeachment shall not extend further than to removal from Office, and disqualification to hold and enjoy any Office of honor, Trust or Profit under the United States: but the Party convicted shall nevertheless be liable and subject to Indictment, Trial, Judgment and Punishment, according to Law.

Section. 4. The Times, Places and Manner of holding Elections for Senators and Representatives, shall be prescribed in each State by the Legislature thereof; but the Congress may at any time by Law make or alter such Regulations, except as to the Places of chusing Senators.

The Congress shall assemble at least once in every Year, and such Meeting shall be on the first Monday in December, unless they shall by Law appoint a different Day.

Section. 5. Each House shall be the Judge of the Elections, Returns and Qualifications of its own Members, and a Majority of each shall constitute a Quorum to do Business; but a smaller Number may adjourn from day to day, and may be authorized to compel the Attendance of absent Members, in such Manner, and under such Penalties as each House may provide.

Each House may determine the Rules of its Proceedings, punish its Members for disorderly Behaviour, and, with the Concurrence of two thirds, expel a Member.

Each House shall keep a Journal of its Proceedings, and from time to time publish the same, excepting such Parts as may in their Judgment require Secrecy; and the Yeas and Nays of the Members of either House on any question shall, at the Desire of one fifth of those Present, be entered on the Journal.

Neither House, during the Session of Congress, shall, without the Consent of the other, adjourn for more than three days, nor to any other Place than that in which the two Houses shall be sitting.

Section. 6. The Senators and Representatives shall receive a Compensation for their Services, to be ascertained by Law, and paid out of the Treasury of the United States. They shall in all Cases, except Treason, Felony and Breach of the Peace, be privileged from Arrest during their Attendance at the Session of their respective Houses, and in going to and returning from the same; and for any Speech or Debate in either House, they shall not be questioned in any other Place.

No Senator or Representative shall, during the Time for which he was elected, be appointed to any civil Office under the Authority of the United States, which shall have been created, or the Emoluments whereof shall have been encreased during such time; and no Person holding any Office under the United States, shall be a Member of either House during his Continuance in Office.

Section. 7. All Bills for raising Revenue shall originate in the House of Representatives; but the Senate may propose or concur with Amendments as on other Bills.

Every Bill which shall have passed the House of Representatives and the Senate, shall, before it become a Law, be presented to the President of the

The US Constitution is the oldest constitution still in use in the world today, and it has been a template for other countries' governing documents.

taxation, the status of citizens and slaves, and other key issues that stood before the country. The result of their work was the Constitution, a document that has lived on for over two centuries and guided a nation that, when the document was written, was still only imagined by the architects of the state.

This speaks to one of the foundations of the Constitution: the system of checks and balances. The founders who wrote the Constitution designed it to allow no one branch of government — the legislative, executive, or judicial — to take more control over the levers of power, ensuring the country would remain resilient in the face of challenges or autocratic leaders. It also provided the people opportunities to vote for their leaders and to hold all representatives, from the president to members of the House of Representatives, accountable.

This resource uses project-based learning, through exit projects, to explore what the Constitution is, how it came to be, and what questions remain about the place of the document in modern American life. Exit projects are designed so that middle-school students can show the entirety of their knowledge on one subject before entering into high school. But exit projects require creativity and critical thinking, and so these projects are designed to serve only as guides as students embark on their own work.

COLONIAL AMERICA

The United States' roots — and the roots of the Constitution — can be traced back to the early 1600s, when the British began colonizing North America with the establishment of Jamestown, in modern Virginia. Established by the Virginia Company and

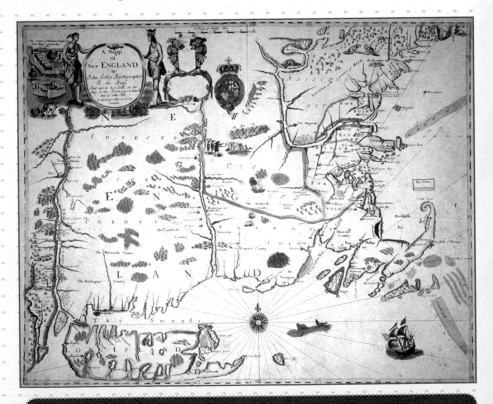

The colonies that would become the United States were established by the British. In the South their focus was agriculture, while in the North religious freedom motivated settlement.

granted the land by the British monarchy, Jamestown began after unsuccessful attempts to create communities in the area, including the Roanoke settlement. At the same time, north of Jamestown, the Pilgrims in the Plymouth Colony were establishing their own community from around 1620. Their community was deeply religious and rooted in a desire to establish a morally superior nation separate from England, as opposed to the economically motivated Virginia Company. These two strands of history are what came together in the earliest days of American history as states were established to govern specific areas. Although still overseen by the king of England, the colonies began to form their own distinct cultures, rooted in innovation, a lack of aristocracy, and Enlightenment values. By the mid-1700s, tensions between colonists and those who governed them in England would boil over into all-out revolution, from which the United States would emerge.

NATIVE AMERICANS

The Colonial period in what would become the United States was marked by foreign rule at the hands of the British, but it was also a period of conquest by colonists over the indigenous populations. Tribes of indigenous peoples were widespread in New England when British colonists settled the area, with wide-ranging customs, ways of life, and alliances among tribes. But colonists disrupted the systems that existed and, rather than finding ways to live with the native populations, began to fight against them. Disease ravaged tribes, leaving millions dead from smallpox and other communicable diseases brought by Europeans. In 1675, colonists waged war against native tribes during King Philip's War, a one-year conflict that killed thousands of indigenous peoples. Although some colonies and communities established trade with tribes, war against indigenous peoples was one of the authorities retained by colonial legislatures, and conflict with Native Americans was the norm as colonists oversaw the expansion of European territory.

QUESTION 1 WHAT DIFFERENT FORMS OF GOVERNMENT EXISTED IN THE COLONIES BEFORE INDEPENDENCE?

Although ruled by the English monarchy, the colonies had some autonomy and were governed in different ways during the century before independence. Each of the original thirteen colonies had a charter, or an agreement between the colony and the English government that recognized the colony's obligations and rights as living under the British Crown. Colonies also had independent legislatures elected by landowning males and a governor appointed by the king. In some states, such as Massachusetts, there was also a strong sense of community involvement, and town halls and meetings were held throughout the colony even after it gained a royal charter. These local governments handled domestic matters specific to their colony, while foreign affairs and taxation were handled by the British government in London.

Colonies had similarly designed governments but differing priorities. Religious freedom was one issue on which states differed. Massachusetts, for example, followed religious doctrine according to the Puritans, while Rhode Island advocated religious freedom in response to the policies of the Puritans. Quakers in

Pennsylvania are an example of how these views could impact other areas. Pennsylvania was established as a pacifist colony and in 1780 would become the second state (after Vermont) to abolish slavery.

Over time, given the changing priorities of the colonies and differing relationships with the British government among elites within the colonies, these governments began to diverge in how they legislated. The tensions between trade, religious identity, taxation, and even colony size would become issues that defined the Constitution.

PROJECT 1
FORMING LOCAL GOVERNMENTS

Create a presentation of the chronology of government of two Colonial governments from 1692 to 1776, comparing and contrasting the way the legislature worked with the governor and what priorities each colony had.

- Choose any two of the original thirteen colonies. These are Connecticut, Delaware, Georgia, Maryland, Massachusetts, New Hampshire, New Jersey, New York, North Carolina, Pennsylvania, Rhode Island, South Carolina, and Virginia.
- Using the internet or your school library, research each of your colonies' history.
  - Who founded the colony? Were there earlier groups of colonists who organized their community?
  - What were some of the reasons your colony was founded? This could be for religious freedom, natural resources, or other reasons. Look for primary

Create a presentation that will help you and your classmates understand the differences between the colonies and how they were governed.

documents by founders or residents, including diaries, letters, or published pamphlets.

o When did the colony receive a royal charter?

o What was the colony's relationship with England? How did the colony's legislature and governor work together?

o How did the colony's unique priorities and identity manifest in the laws its legislature put in place?

o When did rebellion begin manifesting in the colony? Was the colony an early advocate for independence, or did residents feel staying under British rule was beneficial?

o How did early acts against British rule shape the development of the colony?

• Using an online tool or materials on hand, create a presentation that explains the similarities and differences between the Colonial governments you studied.

o Be sure to include the history of each colony, the priorities of that colony, and how each of these influenced the way it developed.

QUESTION 2 WHAT ROLE DID TAXATION PLAY IN SHAPING THE AMERICAN REVOLUTION?

Taxation of the colonies was one of the driving forces behind the American Revolution, serving as an example of the unfair rule imposed by the British. Although represented by a local legislature, which handled domestic issues, the British monarchy still set taxes for the colonies and didn't give them representation in Parliament. This meant that the colonists had no direct way of having a say in matters that governed their lives, business, or foreign affairs.

Taxes alone were not the issue for colonists. They were taxed at a lower rate than those living in Great Britain, and additional taxes weren't enacted until the mid-1700s. But as war debt began to mount, the British government sought Colonial taxes to help offset costs. A 1764 tax on sugar products, called the Sugar Act, was one of the first significant revisions to taxation of the colonies, followed a year later by the controversial Stamp Act

Although the Boston Tea Party was a turning point in Colonial resistance to the British, it came after years of increasing tensions and efforts to fight against British rule.

of 1765, which imposed a tax on paper items. The Stamp Act, which was replaced in 1767 with the Townshend Acts, drew ire and protest by the colonists. It marked a shift in how the colonies related to Britain and led to the organization of resistance that would culminate in the Boston Tea Party in 1773 and revolution in 1775.

For colonists, the issue was taxation without representation, which became a rallying cry for those who resisted British rule. Without a voice in government, the colonists felt it was unfair to tax them at higher and higher rates—even if those rates remained relatively low compared to other British citizens. The roots of American concern over representation in government can be found in this early manifestation of unrest.

PROJECT 2
A REVOLUTION BEGINS

Research the Boston Tea Party and give a presentation on the event, highlighting the impact it had on the revolution.

- **Using the internet or your school library, research the Boston Tea Party.**

Digitized records can provide primary documents or analysis that might otherwise be difficult to find, adding necessary context to your research.

- o What tax acts were enacted before 1773? How did the colonists react to these, and how did the British react to their actions?
- o Who were the Sons of Liberty? What actions did they take before the Boston Tea Party to protest British rule?
- o How did colonies organize on a legislative level against British taxes?
- o What tax act led to the Boston Tea Party, and what took place in Boston Harbor?
- o What other protests took place in other colonies?
- o Why is the Boston Tea Party considered a turning point in the run-up to the American Revolution?
- Using poster board and other materials, make a poster about the Boston Tea Party.
  - o Include a timeline that shows what took place before and after the Tea Party to provide context.
  - o Include information about who took part, what other protests took place around the colonies, and what impact the Tea Party had on politics in the colonies.

WRITING THE CONSTITUTION

The Constitution is the document that laid the foundation for our country, but it wasn't the first that provided a vision for how the postrevolutionary state should function. In 1777, the Articles of Confederation were sent to the thirteen colonies for ratification, which took place in early 1781. From 1777 to 1788,

The Philadelphia Convention brought together prominent leaders from across the colonies and took into account numerous concerns and issues regarding the new country.

the Articles of Confederation served as our Constitution, laying out the rights and responsibilities of the federal government as being those that once belonged to the British monarchy and Parliament. But the Articles of Confederation gave the federal government few practical powers, particularly in regard to domestic security. It became clear that a stronger federal government was needed. As a result, in 1787 the Philadelphia Convention brought together leaders from the colonies, except Rhode Island, to write a new governing document. The result, our Constitution, was ratified and implemented in 1789.

THE CONTINENTAL CONGRESS

Before the passage of the Constitution, the colonies and states were organized in what was called the Continental Congress. This body, which was made up of representatives from all thirteen colonies, was formed in 1774 following punishment passed by the British after the Boston Tea Party. The Continental Congress was spearheaded by Benjamin Franklin and was meant as a way for the colonies to organize and protest what they called the Intolerable Acts. But in 1775, the Revolutionary War began, and the Continental Congress became the de facto government for the newly declared independent United States. The Continental Congress became known as the Confederation Congress, after the Articles of Confederation, following the Revolutionary War. Under this name, it continued to serve as the governing body of the country, until the Constitution was ratified and created the federal government as we know it today.

QUESTION 3 WHAT VALUES FORMED THE BASIS OF THE US CONSTITUTION?

The US Constitution is grounded in values and ideas that come from many sources and work to create a fair and equal society. Those values were first articulated in the Declaration of Independence, which was written in 1776 during the Second Continental Congress. The title is literal; it served as notice to Great Britain that the colonies no longer considered themselves under British rule. The Fourth of July is celebrated as Independence Day because it was on that date in 1776 that the Declaration of Independence was approved.

The Declaration of Independence is just one page, but in it we can find the roots of our democracy and national identity. The preamble famously invokes the "unalienable Rights, that among these are Life, Liberty and the pursuit of Happiness." It goes on to list the wrongdoings and transgressions of the British government that justified the rebellion and to declare the thirteen colonies independent.

Although far from explicit, the Declaration of Independence invokes rights that would go on to form the basis of our democracy. The preamble highlights the idea that "all men are created equal," while the document denounces the British for things like taxation without representation. While these ideals were not always held to, they were integral to the foundation of the United States. The preamble also provides the precedent that the colonies, though independent states, have a mutual obligation to work together and protect one another, something that would eventually feed into the federal government.

Studying the Constitution can give us a new understanding of the history of our country, the values that defined the times in which our country was founded, and the vision the founders had for the nation.

PROJECT 3
THE BASIS OF A NEW GOVERNMENT

Identify the values underpinning the Declaration of Independence and find the ways in which they are put into action in the Constitution.

- **Using the internet or your school library, identify at least three values that are included in the Declaration of Independence.**

- o What are values in the context of government? What were some of the values that the colonists held that found their way into the Declaration of Independence?
- o You can find values throughout the document. Consider what rationalization the document provides for declaring independence. What do these indictments say about the values of this new nation?
- o Are the values you selected linked in any way? How do they inform or contrast with one another?
- Look for your values in the Constitution. It might not be easy to find them spelled out, so consider the meaning and importance of the values you selected.
  - o How do values become policy?
  - o What sorts of policies do we find in the Constitution that reflect the values you identified?
- Using an online tool or hands-on materials, create a presentation that compares the values you found in the Declaration of Independence with how they manifest in the Constitution.
  - o Be sure to include what the Constitution tells us about the values of the early United States and the colonies.
  - o Are there any historical cases that work against the idea that these values were equally applied? For example, how can a nation based on the equality of "all men" maintain a system of slavery?

QUESTION 4 WHY DID THE FOUNDING FATHERS INTRODUCE THE BILL OF RIGHTS?

The Constitution was ratified by the necessary nine colonies in 1788, but it was a long and hard fight to ensure that all signatories felt comfortable putting their names to the document and that the additional four colonies eventually signed on. In fact, immediately after the ratification of the Constitution, ten amendments were proposed to address concerns raised by those who advocated limits on federal power. These would become known as the Bill of Rights, and they were intended to provide protections for freedom and liberty.

James Madison began working on the amendments in 1789, using the Virginia Declaration of Rights (written in 1776 by George Mason) as a template and adding freedom of the press and the right to a trial by jury, among others. But he also asked for suggestions from the states themselves, ensuring that many voices were heard. The amendments, which were proposed originally as nine

James Madison was a key figure in the drafting of the Constitution and the amendments that became the Bill of Rights.

alterations, were meant to safeguard individual rights from the federal government, an addition to the Constitution's focus on governmental structure.

The process to pass and ratify the amendments was long and difficult, with many changes taking place. Many, particularly Federalists, were worried that altering the Constitution would weaken federal power and set a precedent that could easily be manipulated by future politicians. It wasn't until late 1791 that Congress approved and all states ratified the Bill of Rights. Although today we still debate the place and importance of amendments, the government has only passed seventeen more since 1791, and the flexibility the amendment mechanism provides is crucial for the evolution of our country.

PROJECT 4
GUARANTEEING OUR RIGHTS

With a partner, write a dialogue that uses quotes by the Founding Fathers to imagine what it was like to write the First Amendment.

- Using the internet or your school library, research the writing of the Bill of Rights.
  - o Find primary documents and quotes from the Founding Fathers, including Thomas Jefferson, George Washington, and James Madison, that speak to the need for or the process of writing the First Amendment.
  - o What problems arose that required the Bill of Rights? What gaps in the Constitution were they intended to fill? What specifically did the First Amendment mean for the new government?

o What were the concerns raised by those who didn't want to amend the Constitution? What did they worry it would mean for the future of the Constitution?

o Consider writings from 1788 to 1791. What can these writings tell us about the process of writing the Bill of Rights? How did attitudes and ideas about the Bill of Rights change during that time?

- With a partner, choose two Founding Fathers who helped write the Bill of Rights. One of you should be James Madison, while the other can be another influential individual in the process.

o Write a dialogue between them, making reference to the inspirations, issues, and process of writing the Bill of Rights. Imagine you are writing the First Amendment. How does what you have learned about the Bill of Rights apply to this particular amendment?

o To include more voices, you can make reference to other people who played a role in writing the Bill of Rights by quoting them in your conversation.

o Be sure to include a range of ideas and issues that you learned about during your research.

A MORE PERFECT UNION

When it was written in the late 1780s, the Constitution was a revolutionary document. Although other similar documents had been introduced in legislatures and governments throughout history, the US Constitution represented a break

The United States has a wealth of documents and writings related to the founding of our country, providing insight into the Constitution.

with governing methods of old. Drawing from sources from the ancient world to the Enlightenment to the unique experiences of the colonies, it was a thoroughly modern example of how to create a nation. But the document itself is strikingly short and at times vague, giving rise to the ongoing debate about what the founders intended. Centuries later, experts continue to closely read and interpret the Constitution, coming back with multiple ways of understanding our foundational national text.

QUESTION 5 ACCORDING TO THE PREAMBLE, WHAT ARE THE GOALS OF THE CONSTITUTION?

With just seven articles, the Constitution sets out to achieve a great deal in a relatively short amount of space. Few sections of the document showcase the ability of the founders to do just that better than the Preamble. In just one sentence, the preamble outlines the goals and rationale for the Constitution and is considered an iconic representation of what the United States stands for. It reads:

> **We the People of the United States, in Order to form a more perfect Union, establish Justice, insure domestic Tranquility, provide for the common defence, promote the general Welfare, and secure the Blessings of Liberty to ourselves and our Posterity, do ordain and establish this Constitution of the United States of America.**

The preamble gives us an overview of what the Constitution sets out to do, and it can help us understand the importance of the articles that follow.

PROJECT 5
THE DREAM OF A COUNTRY

Select one goal noted in the preamble and find examples in the Constitution that support it to create a presentation.

- From the preamble above, identify and choose one goal.
- Using the internet or your school library, research that goal.
  - o What was the context in which this was written? What made your goal important enough to be included in the Constitution?
  - o What might that goal mean in practice? What kinds of policies should we look for in the Constitution to identify the manifestation of this goal?

Working with a partner or group can help you find new angles, ideas, and perspectives on the Constitution and US history.

- Read the Constitution and identify instances in which your goal is represented. This could be in specific responsibilities, in checks on power, or in duties of office.
  - For example, "the common defence" can be found in sections that deal with declaring war or signing treaties.
  - How do these policies represent the goal you identified?
  - Is there any controversy around the goal or the policies you identified?
- Using an online tool or materials you have on hand, create a presentation that explains the relationship between your goal in the preamble and specific policies in the Constitution.
  - Show how goals manifest in the Constitution as policy.
  - Be sure to include any controversy or checks and balances that influence the way these policies are implemented, or other interesting information you find.

QUESTION 6 HOW DOES THE CONSTITUTION DIVIDE THE JOB OF GOVERNING THE COUNTRY BETWEEN THE BRANCHES OF GOVERNMENT?

The writers of the Constitution considered it extremely important to ensure the federal government did not gain outsized power, which would make it easy to rule over the people in undemocratic ways. But in order to do this, it took more than enshrining voting rights. The founders created a system that keeps all parts of government from gaining too much power. This system uses checks and balances to ensure that no one branch of government is able to govern without the consent and help of the other two branches, and it has become a hallmark of our democracy.

The Constitution divides the powers of government between the three branches—the legislative, the executive, and the judicial. The legislature is Congress, and it is tasked with drafting and passing laws. The executive branch, which includes the president and the president's cabinet, implements these laws. The judicial branch, including the Supreme Court, rules on the legality of these laws and hears challenges to them on the grounds of the Constitution. Within that simple division are more complex relationships; for example, after Congress passes a bill, the president must sign it before it can become a law. On the other hand, the president has to get approval from Congress to nominate Supreme Court justices or members of the cabinet.

This system is complex, and throughout history loopholes have emerged. Executive orders, for example, give the president a way to enact policies without

The branches of government established by the Constitution are designed to provide checks and balances on one another, so that all branches must work together.

congressional approval. But these are still subject to judicial oversight and can be blocked by federal courts. Although this can make the process of governing long and difficult, it is an important safeguard for democracy.

PROJECT 6
PROTECTING POWER

Make a diorama showing the checks and balances, as well as differing roles, of each branch of government.

- Using the internet or your school library, research checks and balances and the roles of each branch of government.
  - o What are the sole responsibilities of the legislative, judicial, and executive branches? What do these responsibilities say about the work done by each branch?
  - o Where do their responsibilities intersect?
  - o What are the ways each branch oversees the work of the other two?
- Using an online tool or materials on hand, create a poster that shows the responsibilities of each branch and how each functions in the checks and balances system.
  - o One way to do this is to break your poster into three sections—one for each branch of government.
  - o Include information that is both specific to each branch and related to all three.

QUESTION 7 WHAT IS THE RELATIONSHIP BETWEEN THE FEDERAL GOVERNMENT AND THE STATES ACCORDING TO THE US CONSTITUTION?

The relationship between the states and the federal government was an important point of debate among the writers and signatories of the Constitution. Under the colonial system, colonies had independent legislatures that handled domestic matters, and the federal government was originally envisioned as handling only matters that were foreign in nature. But as the government developed and the writers of the Constitution worked, it became clear that a stronger federal government was needed. This created conflict with those who felt the federal government, particularly through matters of representation, could overpower the local governments of smaller states.

INTERNATIONAL RELATIONS

Under the original Articles of Confederation, the federal government was given the duties once held by the British government—meaning it was primarily responsible for international affairs. The Constitution maintained this federal responsibility for managing relations with foreign countries and waging war; states are not able to set trade deals that go against federal policy with outside countries, nor can they invade or befriend states without the federal government. But the way the federal government manages international affairs is not clear in the Constitution, which has created tension. Although there are duties held by both the legislative and executive branch, with overlap on issues like formally declaring war and ratifying international treaties, international relations are mostly governed by changing norms. For example, the president has gained significant authority during wartimes, which has made it possible for the executive branch to begin a war without congressional approval.

To settle the debate, the bicameral Congress was created to ensure small and large states have equal say in the laws of the country, and the Electoral College was given weighted representation in the election of the president. States were also given specific rights and responsibilities by the Constitution. Although the federal government and the Supreme Court set the laws of the land, states are given significant freedom in setting domestic priorities and policy.

The relationship between the federal government and states was particularly complicated when the state in question was located far from the capital. These states, such as California and Texas, developed in ways that emphasized independence and local governance, which was at times at odds with federal priorities. What's more, the geographic differences between states meant that what was considered important or necessary for a state like Illinois was not the same as for a state like Nevada. This is why state control of some matters is so important; it allows states the opportunity to do what is best for them based on their resources and needs.

PROJECT 7
A GROWING COUNTRY

Research and present how geography impacted a state joining the Union after the Constitution.

- Using the internet or your school library, research the process by which a state becomes part of the United States.
  - o Research the admission to the union clause, found in Article IV, Section 3, Clause 1. What are the requirements for states that want to join the Union?
  - o What is the process by which the government hears and approves states that want to be in the Union?
  - o What roles does each branch of government play in the process of admitting a state to the union?
- Choose one state outside of the original thirteen colonies that has been admitted to the Union. This can be your own state if it was admitted after 1788 or another that you find interesting.
  - o When was it admitted to the Union?
  - o What was the historical context surrounding its admission?
  - o How was the area settled, and why did the government want to include it in the United States? Consider finding primary documents to find this information.
  - o What is the climate of your state? Does it have extreme geography? How did this impact the way it was settled, the resources the settlers had access to, and early laws?
  - o What was required of this state to become part of the Union?
  - o What was the process like for the state, on both a local and federal level? Was there any controversy in its admission to the Union?
- Using an online tool or materials on hand, create a presentation that explains the chronology of your state

Draw on a variety of resources while working on your project to ensure you are basing your research on a diverse range of voices.

joining the Union, what it needed to do to become a state, and why the country wanted to admit it.

o   Be sure to include information about both the state-level and federal-level process, and highlight any conflict between the two levels of government.

o   Include information related to the impact of geography. Was the geography of a state, such as Alaska, an important part of why it became a state? Did climate, like in the Southwest, impact its settlement?

CHAPTER FOUR

THE LEGISLATIVE BRANCH

The role and responsibilities of the legislative branch are laid out in Article I of the Constitution, and it is the most thoroughly discussed branch of government within the document. It's

Our modern legislative branch was born out of a compromise between those who wanted equal representation and proportional representation for states.

easy to imagine why; the legislature was one of the most hotly debated issues at the Philadelphia Convention and a bone of contention between political factions in the years after the Revolutionary War. Congress, our legislature, is the result of the Connecticut Compromise, designed to incorporate ideas from both Federalists and Anti-Federalists. It is made up of the Senate and the House of Representatives, and it includes both proportional representation and equal representation. The two houses work together on legislation, government policy, and state-level issues that reflect national debates.

PRESIDENT OF THE SENATE

Although much attention is paid to the way the president and Congress interact, one of the most interesting and important overlaps between the executive and legislative branches is actually the role of the vice president. The vice president is part of both branches, serving as a deputy to the president and as president of the Senate. In this role, the vice president is responsible for swearing in senators, announcing the results of votes, presiding during joint sessions of Congress, and casting tie-breaking votes on bills. The president of the Senate does not often take part in the goings-on of the Senate as a show of respect for the independence of the legislature, but the role can carry serious impact, allowing contentious bills or appointments to move forward when the Senate is divided.

QUESTION 8 ACCORDING TO THE CONSTITUTION, HOW DO THE TWO HOUSES OF THE LEGISLATIVE BRANCH INTERACT?

The Senate and the House of Representatives are different in several important ways. Although all members of Congress are elected by direct elections in their states, the sizes of each body are different. The Senate is made up of one hundred members, or two from each state, who are elected to six-year terms. The House is made up of 435 members and 6 nonvoting members, all elected for two-year terms. Representatives are voted on and represent specific state districts, and the number allocated to each state is based on the census to ensure proportional representation based on population.

Congress is responsible for passing laws, overseeing and approving budgetary and financial policy, approving presidential nominations, and advising the president on matters ranging from foreign affairs to domestic initiatives. Congress also has final say on the formal declaration of war and signing of foreign treaties, a check on presidential authority around the world. Through committees, Congress studies and reports on matters of national importance and conducts hearings to investigate issues ranging from potentially criminal acts by the government to subjects related to advocacy.

Congress divides powers between both bodies in varying ways, which requires the legislature to work together on most duties. Although both bodies work independently in most cases, matters like legislation have to pass both bodies before they can be sent to the president for final signing. Other duties, such as impeachment, or formally declaring wrongdoing on the part of a public official, give specific duties to both bodies that have significant importance. The House brings the case for impeachment, while the Senate tries the case.

PROJECT 8
PASSING LAWS

Create a map that follows the path of a bill through Congress.

- Using the internet or your school library, research the process by which a bill becomes a law.
  - o Bills can be introduced in both the House and the Senate. What are the procedures by which bills are brought forward and voted on? Are there ways in which senators and representatives can block a hearing or vote on a bill?
  - o What is the procedure by which a bill, if passed, is sent to the other body of Congress?
  - o Is it possible for either body to change a bill once it has been passed by one body?
  - o After each body of Congress has passed a bill, it goes into reconciliation. What is that process, and why is it important?
  - o What happens when a bill is sent to the president? What happens if the bill is vetoed? Can Congress override a veto?
- Using an online tool or materials on hand, create a "map" that shows how a bill passes through Congress.
  - o You can make up your own bill or use one that was passed and re-create its progress.
  - o Decide if you want your bill to originate in the House or the Senate. Bills that originate in the House are prefaced with HR, while bills that originate in the Senate are prefaced with S.
  - o To create your map, use the House or Senate as a

starting point, then show all the "stops" a bill makes on the way to becoming a law.

o Consider including dates or a time frame to show how much time can pass between stages of the process. You can also include obstacles and how they can be overcome for a bill to become a law.

QUESTION 9 WHAT SPECIFIC BUDGETARY POWERS ARE GRANTED TO CONGRESS?

Congress holds powers ranging from taxation to international affairs. The relationship between Congress and the executive branch is complex because of the overlap of powers between the two. Although the president is the commander in chief of the armed forces, Congress is responsible for declaring war and raising the army and navy. Congress is responsible for all taxation and bills related to financial policy, but the president creates a budget proposal for each year, marking the ways in which the administration feels funds should be allocated. Bills originate in Congress but require presidential approval in order to become laws. Although the president selects nominees for the cabinet and the Supreme Court, Congress must approve them before they can take office.

This give-and-take is important. It ensures communication and cooperation between these two branches of government, but it can also give rise to conflict and gridlock. If communication or cooperation breaks down between the executive and legislative branches, then we see legislation come to a standstill, which can lead to issues such as government shutdowns.

Although the relationship between Congress and the president is outlined in some detail by the Constitution, it is norms that keep either branch from using its full power to obstruct the other. These unwritten rules are just as important as those in the Constitution and play an important role in ensuring our government functions effectively and efficiently.

PROJECT 9
LEVYING TAXES

Research and present an example of Congress levying taxes.

- Using the internet or your school library, research how Congress levies taxes.
  - o What does it mean to levy taxes?
  - o What limitations are put on the power to levy taxes?
  - o Does Congress share this power with any other governmental body?
  - o Find one time in history when this power was used.
    - For example, when did Congress first impose taxes at a national level?
- Using an online tool or materials on hand, create a presentation about a particular tax.
  - o Include the importance of this tax, why it was imposed, and the process by which it was put into practice.
  - o Be sure to include information about the power of Congress to levy taxes generally so that you can show what this power means in practice and any other historical context that has shaped the way we understand this power.

CHAPTER FIVE

THE EXECUTIVE BRANCH

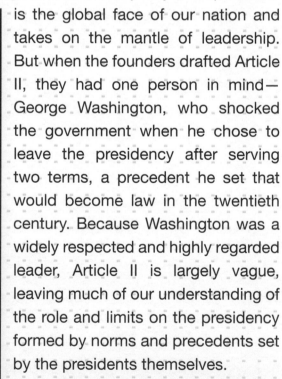

Article II of the Constitution lays out the duties and responsibilities of the executive branch, specifically the president. This branch is perhaps the most highly visible in our government. Although limited in many ways, the president is the global face of our nation and takes on the mantle of leadership. But when the founders drafted Article II, they had one person in mind— George Washington, who shocked the government when he chose to leave the presidency after serving two terms, a precedent he set that would become law in the twentieth century. Because Washington was a widely respected and highly regarded leader, Article II is largely vague, leaving much of our understanding of the role and limits on the presidency formed by norms and precedents set by the presidents themselves.

The US presidency was designed with George Washington in mind, and his time in office set numerous precedents we still associate with the leader of the country.

STATE OF THE UNION

Each year, the president is expected to appear before a joint session of Congress to give a speech intended to offer an overview of the accomplishments of the year before, the challenges facing the country, and a vision for moving forward. This is called the State of the Union address, and it is enshrined in the Constitution under Article II, Section 3, Clause 1. The event has become one of the most important on the political landscape, with significant media coverage. It is a formal occasion. A written invitation must be extended by the Speaker of the House, and everything from the number of guests to the process for the president to enter the Capitol is mandated by precedent and policy. The speech itself can be long or short, but it is expected to give insight into the direction in which the president hopes legislation will move over the coming year.

QUESTION 10 WHAT IS THE ELECTORAL COLLEGE, AND WHAT WERE THE INTENTIONS OF THE FOUNDERS IN CREATING IT?

Every four years, eligible voters go to the polls to cast their vote for the president of the United States. But it may surprise you that when the returns come in and the news reports on the winner, the election isn't technically over. That comes in December, a month or more after the ballots have been cast, when the Electoral College meets to formally elect the next president.

The Electoral College was created to safeguard the vote. It was a compromise between those who wanted Congress to elect the president and those who called for direct election. Under the process, each state is given a number of electors equal to its representation in Congress, ensuring that even small states have a significant impact on the election. It is also designed to protect the election from candidates deemed unsuitable. Although the system has moved away from playing a goalkeeping function, it was intended that electors could block a candidate from taking office.

The Electoral College has become a controversial issue in politics today, with some arguing it should be replaced by direct election via the popular vote. This is for several reasons. Today we know the popular vote totals almost immediately, making it easier and highly accurate to use that as the sole metric in elections. What's more, as states have moved to systems that penalize electors for voting against the popular vote in their state, the intended purpose of the Electoral College has been undermined or eradicated. But advocates believe it is an important facet of democracy and a tradition worth maintaining that ensures rural or small states have equal say in an election.

PROJECT 10
SAFEGUARDING DEMOCRACY

Using primary sources, create a presentation that uses original quotes from the founders to explain the role of the Electoral College.

- **Using the internet or your school library, research the Electoral College.**
  - o **What were the differing viewpoints that led to it being introduced?**

44

o What were the concerns that made the Electoral College necessary? How does it address these concerns?

o How did the founders see the role of the Electoral College in elections? Use primary documents to find quotes from founders such as Alexander Hamilton and James Madison about the Electoral College.

- Using an online tool or materials on hand, create a presentation that includes the role of the Electoral College, why it was created, and what the Founding Fathers thought it meant for democracy.

o Include original quotes in each part of the presentation to provide context, but be sure to explain who said them and why.

QUESTION 11 WHAT DID THE FOUNDERS INTEND FOR THE EXECUTIVE BRANCH WHEN THEY WROTE THE CONSTITUTION?

The Constitution's Article II is vague and short compared to other articles, leading to confusion on what the founders hoped for out of the presidency and the executive branch. Section 1 of Article II simply opens, "Executive Power shall be vested in the President of the United States of America." Only three sections enumerate the office's powers, a surprisingly short outline given the importance of the office. That lack of detail has given rise to norms and precedents that govern the role of the president, which are unwritten rules most officeholders abide.

According to James Madison's writings on the Philadelphia Convention, there was limited debate about the scope and power of the presidency. George Washington was the leader of the Congress, and all leaders expected him to become the first president under the new Constitution. The role they were crafting was unlike any other in government in the Western world, and they didn't necessarily envision it to be as powerful as it has become.

The power we associate with the presidency can also be traced back to Washington, a charismatic and powerful leader who exerted restraint even with the vague parameters of the office he held for two terms. But the model of norms we expect our leaders to follow can be problematic, since breaking them does not necessary violate law. Take, for example, the presidency of Franklin D. Roosevelt. After serving two terms, which had become customary following Washington's decision to step down after serving eight years as president, Roosevelt ran for a third and fourth, winning both times. This led to an amendment that put into law what had been a foregone conclusion regarding presidential term limits. Other norms, including deference to Congress or other bodies, could be violated in similar ways with little by way of accountability.

PROJECT 11
WHAT MAKES A LEADER?

Using primary sources and quotes, act out with a partner a debate between the founders about what the presidency should be and what leadership qualities they saw as important to the office.

- Using the internet or your school library, research Article II of the Constitution.
  - o What was the context for the writing of the article? Who took part in the debates?

The limits of the presidency have been defined by those who hold the office, such as the introduction of term limits following the four elections of President Franklin D. Roosevelt.

o What were the dominant ideas about the way the presidency should function?

o What was George Washington's role in writing the article?

o What qualities in Washington did the early leaders of the United States value? What other values or qualities did they think a president should have, and did they work to build those qualities into the office?

o How did Washington's time in office influence the way we understand the presidency? What did he add to the office that is not in the Constitution?

o What are some of the advantages and disadvantages of the way the office is outlined in the Constitution? Think about what you have learned in your research, read about what scholars say about the office, and consider how the founders believed the office should function.

o Be sure to find original quotes from primary documents to include.

- With a partner, write a dialogue that shows the way Article II was debated and written.

o One of you should be in favor of a strong presidency, while the other favors a weaker presidency.

o Include debate about what makes a good leader, including the qualities one should look for in a president.

o Include original quotes from the founders and those who took part in the debate.

CHAPTER SIX

THE JUDICIAL BRANCH

The judicial branch is laid out in Article III, which is also relatively short. But this is in part because the role of the judiciary—or the courts—is straightforward. The Supreme Court and the network of federal courts around the country are responsible for hearing cases in which the

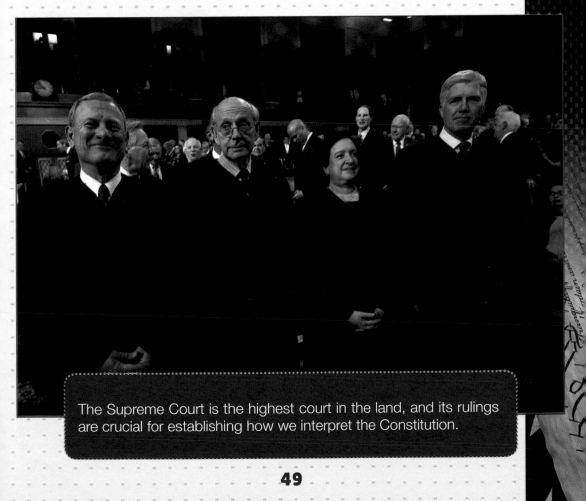

The Supreme Court is the highest court in the land, and its rulings are crucial for establishing how we interpret the Constitution.

constitutionality of a law is called into question, such as on matters of civil rights. These courts also hear cases in which the United States is a defendant or plaintiff, or in which a foreign country is involved. Not all such cases make it to the Supreme Court, which is responsible for hearing a select few cases each year. The court's rulings set precedents that can have a lasting impact on how the Constitution is interpreted and how other court rulings are decided. Therefore, Supreme Court rulings often hinge on small parts of larger laws, making its decisions highly specific despite their wide-ranging impact.

CHOOSING JUSTICES

The selection of Supreme Court justices is one of the few instances in which Congress and the executive branch have influence over the court. The Supreme Court is currently made up of nine justices, with one serving as chief justice. The other eight are considered associate justices. All of them are nominated by the president, and they have to be approved by Congress before being appointed to a lifetime tenure on the court. The Supreme Court is intended to be nonpartisan, rooting its rulings in constitutional law rather than personal ideology. But within the field of constitutional law, there are many interpretations of the Constitution, and which one a justice leans toward can influence the way he or she rules. What's more, there is no legal stipulation for how many justices can sit on the court at one time, meaning that only the norm of having nine justices at one time has stopped sitting presidents from expanding the court.

QUESTION 12 WHAT STRUCTURE DOES THE JUDICIAL BRANCH TAKE?

The judiciary is made up of many courts around the country that interact in differing ways. All the courts hear civilian or criminal cases that involve the US government or US laws. This could include the violation of civil rights or the state bringing a case against someone who has committed a felony.

The first tier of federal courts are US district courts, which are found around the country. They are considered the first courts in which cases are heard before making their way through the rest of the court system. This takes place through appeals, reaching

The US federal court system is a complex network that spans the United States and helps ensure that justice remains a central value within the country.

the US circuit court of appeals after a panel of judges finds fault with the original ruling at the district court level. From there, a case can be submitted to the Supreme Court, which is the highest court in the land.

The Supreme Court selects cases to hear, rather than hearing any case brought before it. Following oral arguments, the court debates and discusses the case for a long time—sometimes months—before handing down a decision, which is final and cannot be appealed again. Because of the lengthy process to have a case heard by the Supreme Court, it is not uncommon for the media and legal experts to follow cases that originate in the lower courts as possible future cases that the Supreme Court will hear.

PROJECT 12
A NETWORK PRESERVING JUSTICE

Create a map that shows the levels of federal courts and their responsibilities.

- Using the internet or your school library, research the federal judicial system.
  - How are cases brought before the US circuit court? What is required for a case to be within the circuit court jurisdiction?
  - How are cases brought to the appellate courts? How are the panels of judges selected, and what is their role in deciding jurisdiction? Once a case is brought, how does it proceed if the ruling is overturned?
  - What cases are heard by the Supreme Court? How might the justices decide which cases to hear and which not to hear?

o What is the procedure for a case to be heard at the Supreme Court? What takes place after the ruling is handed down? How does the executive branch enforce the ruling?

o How are federal courts spread out around the country? Are they concentrated in cities, or are there courts across each state?

- Using an online tool or materials on hand, create a map that shows how federal courts are situated around the country.

o Include information about the level of court, what its responsibilities are within the system, and how a case works its way from one to another.

- You can choose a case to use as an example that was eventually heard by the Supreme Court, working backward in your research to trace how it got there, or make up a case that fits the jurisdiction of the courts.

QUESTION 13 HOW DOES THE SUPREME COURT WEIGH IN ON LAWS IN THE UNITED STATES?

The Supreme Court upholds the Constitution by ruling on laws that may violate it in ways both large and small. The court hears only cases that are related to the Constitution or laws passed by Congress, meaning that any case that has made it to the Supreme Court is immensely high profile. All cases heard by the Supreme Court are of critical importance to our democracy; some cases in the past have had impact on voting rights, health care access, and marriage equality. But oftentimes the decisions handed down by the courts are highly specific, and it can be difficult to fully understand how the precedents they set impact how we interpret the Constitution.

The Supreme Court serves as an important check on federal power. The court is, essentially, an advocate for the people, ensuring that all laws Congress passes and all actions taken by the president are constitutional. Decisions by the Supreme Court influence the way the government functions, the way states implement laws, and how the public sees itself in relation to the country.

PROJECT 13
THE HIGHEST COURT IN THE LAND

Select one case that has been heard by the Supreme Court and create a presenation about the impact of the court's ruling.

- Using the internet or your school library, find a Supreme Court case you want to learn more about.
- What was the historical significance of the case? What made it an important case for the Supreme Court to hear?
- What was the case about? What was the constitutional challenge the case brought?
- How did the court rule? Was it a unanimous decision, or was the court divided? Be sure to include quotes from both the majority and dissenting justices.
- What precedent did this case set? How did the law change after it was ruled? Did it have any effects beyond legislation?
- Using an online tool or materials on hand, create a presentation that explains the case, why it was important, and the impact it had following the ruling.

AMENDMENT A change or addition, particularly to the Constitution, as approved by all states.

ARTICLES OF CONFEDERATION The first constitution of the United States, which granted very limited powers to the central government.

AUTONOMOUS Self-governing, either fully or to within an agreed framework with a larger body.

BICAMERAL Referring to a legislature with two houses, such as Congress.

BILL OF RIGHTS The first ten amendments to the Constitution, which provide safeguards for fundamental rights.

CONSTITUTION A document that lays out the basic tenets of the state, including restrictions on and the powers of government bodies.

DECLARATION OF INDEPENDENCE The 1776 document that officially announced the separation of the United States from Great Britain, beginning the American Revolution.

DEMOCRACY A form of government in which the people vote for officials, thereby holding them accountable to the will of the public.

EXECUTIVE Referring to the branch of government that is responsible for enforcing laws and includes the president.

FEDERAL Referring to the central government that serves the nation rather than a particular state.

FEDERALIST An early advocate for a strong central government.

INDIGENOUS Native to a given land or area.

JUDICIAL Referring to the branch of government that is responsible for determining the legality of laws and potential violations of them; the courts.

LEGISLATIVE Referring to the branch of government that is responsible for writing and passing laws.

PHILADELPHIA CONVENTION The 1787 meeting at which delegates designed and wrote the Constitution.

PILGRIM A member of an early group of American colonists who sought religious freedom and adhered to a strict interpretation of Christianity.

PRECEDENT An action or legal decision that sets an example for behavior that informs future leaders and officials.

RATIFICATION The passing of a law by all states; a process that is required of any amendment to the Constitution.

STAMP ACT A 1765 tax passed by the British that imposed charges on all printed paper.

American Constitution Society for Law and Policy
1899 L Street NW, Suite 200
Washington, DC 20036
(202) 393-6181
Website: https://www.acslaw.org
Email: info@ACSLaw.org
Twitter: @ACSlaw
This organization works to interpret and spread awareness of the
   US Constitution in the areas of law and policy.

Bill of Rights Institute
1310 N. Courthouse Road, #620
Arlington, VA 22201
(703) 894-1776
Website: https://www.billofrightsinstitute.org
Email: info@billofrightsinstitute.org
Twitter: @BRInstitute
This nonprofit works to educate young people on civil liberties
   and US history, particularly regarding the US Constitution
   and the Bill of Rights.

Center for State Constitutional Studies
Rutgers University–Camden
217 N. Fifth Street, Room 612
Camden, NJ 08102
(856) 225-6625
Website: https://statecon.camden.rutgers.edu

Email: cscs@camden.rutgers.edu

This Rutgers University–based center is dedicated to the study of American state constitutions.

Federalist Society

1776 I Street NW, Suite 300

Washington, DC 2006

(202) 822-8138

Website: https://fedsoc.org

Email: info@fedsoc.org

Facebook: @Federalist.Society

Twitter: @FedSoc

This think tank and policy center advocates for a strict interpretation of the US Constitution, particularly in regard to the principles of limited government.

National Archives and Records Administration

8601 Adelphi Road

College Park, MD 20740-6001

(866) 272-6272

Website: https://www.archives.gov

Twitter: @USNatArchives

This federal resource houses and digitizes documents of national importance, including the Declaration of Independence.

National Center for Constitutional Studies

National Humanities Institute

PO Box 1387

Bowie, MD 20718-1387

(301) 464-4277

Website: http://www.nhinet.org

Email: service@nccs.net
Facebook: @AsktheFounders
Twitter: @CenterNational
This nonprofit organization seeks to raise awareness and education about the Constitution by offering courses and other resources.

National Constitution Center
525 Arch Street
Philadelphia, PA 19106
(215) 409-6600
Website: https://constitutioncenter.org
Email: education@constitutioncenter.org
Twitter: @ConstitutionCtr
This nonprofit organization and museum seeks to raise awareness of and education about the Constitution and US constitutional history.

FOR FURTHER READING

Berkin, Carol. *The Bill of Rights: The Fight to Secure America's Liberties*. New York, NY: Simon & Schuster, 2016.

Hamilton, Alexander. *The Federalist Papers*. New York, NY: Dover Publications, 2014.

Koplin, Amanda. *Understanding Supreme Court Cases*. New York, NY: Rosen Publishing, 2018.

Levinson, Cynthia, and Sanford Levinson. *Fault Lines in the Constitution: The Framers, Their Fights, and the Flaws That Affect Us Today*. Atlanta, GA: Peachtree Publishers, 2017.

Lowery, Zoe. *The American Revolution*. New York, NY: Rosen Publishing, 2016.

Lusted, Marcia Amidon. *The US Constitution*. Mankato, MN: Child's World, 2017.

McAuliffe, Bill. *The US Presidency*. Mankato, MN: Creative Paperbacks, 2017.

McAuliffe, Bill. *The US Senate*. Mankato, MN: Creative Paperbacks, 2017.

Mooney, Carla, and Tom Casteel. *The US Constitution: Discover How Democracy Works*. White River Junction, VT: Nomad Press, 2016.

Steinkraus, Kyla. *Constitution*. Vero Beach, FL: Rourke Educational Media, 2015.

BIBLIOGRAPHY

Bailyn, Bernard. *The Ideological Origins of the American Revolution*. Cambridge, MA: Belknap Press, 2017.

Beeman, Richard. *Plain, Honest Men: The Making of the American Constitution*. New York, NY: Random House Trade Paperbacks, 2010.

Berkin, Carol. *A Brilliant Solution: Inventing the American Constitution*. New York, NY: Mariner Books, 2003.

Berkin, Carol. *A Sovereign People: The Crises of the 1790s and the Birth of American Nationalism*. New York, NY: Basic Books, 2017.

Ferling, John. *A Leap in the Dark: The Struggle to Create the American Republic*. Oxford, UK: Oxford University Press, 2004.

Holton, Woody. *Unruly Americans and the Origins of the Constitution*. New York, NY: Hill & Wang, 2008.

Hoock, Holger. *Scars of Independence: America's Violent Birth*. New York, NY: Crown, 2017.

Klarman, Michael J. *The Framer's Coup: The Making of the United States Constitution*. Oxford, UK: Oxford University Press, 2016.

Stewart, David O. *The Summer of 1787: The Men Who Invented the Constitution*. New York, NY: Simon & Schuster, 2008.

Taylor, Alan. *American Colonies: The Settling of North America*. Vol. 1. New York, NY: Penguin Books, 2002.

Taylor, Alan. *American Revolutions: A Continental History, 1750–1804*. New York NY: W. W. Norton & Company, 2016.

A

Articles of Confederation, 18–19, 32–33

B

Bill of Rights, 23–24
Boston Tea Party, project about, 16–17

C

checks and balances, 8, 29–31
  project about, 31
colonies, 9–10
  early governments of, 11–12
  freedom of religion, 11–12
  list of original thirteen, 12
  reasons for establishing, 10
  taxation of, 14–16
Continental Congress, 19

D

Declaration of Independence, 20
  project about, 21–22

E

Electoral College, 43–44
  project about, 44–45
executive branch, 30, 42, 45
  and Electoral College, 43–45

project about, 46–48
exit projects
  Boston Tea Party, 16–17
  checks and balances, 31
  Declaration of Independence, 21–22
  Electoral College, 44–45
  executive branch, 46–48
  federal courts, 52–53
  First Amendment, 24–25
  local government, 12–14
  passing laws, 39–40
  preamble to US Constitution, 28–29
  states joining Union, 33–35
  Supreme Court, 54
  taxes, 41

F

federal courts
  circuit court of appeals, 51–52
  district, 51
  project about, 52–53
  Supreme Court, 52
federal government, role of, 32–33
First Amendment, project about, 24–25

G

government
  early colonial, 11–12
  local, 12–14

I

indigenous peoples, 10–11

J

Jamestown colony, 9–10
judicial branch, 30, 49–50
   selection of justices, 50

L

legislative branch, 30, 36–37
   bicameral, 33, 37, 38
   passing laws, 39–40
   powers of, 40
   relationship to other branches,
      40–41
   responsibilities of, 38

M

Madison, James, 23, 45–46

P

Philadelphia Convention, 6, 8, 19
Pilgrims, 10
Plymouth colony, 10
preamble to US Constitution, 27
   project about, 28–29

R

Roosevelt, Franklin D., 46

S

Stamp Act, 14–15
State of the Union address, 43

states
   joining the Union, 33–35
   role of, 32, 33
Sugar Tax, 14
Supreme Court
   and Constitution, 53–54
   project about, 54
   selection of justices, 50

T

taxes, 14–16
   project about, 41
   without representation, 14, 15–16
Townshend Acts, 15

U

US Constitution
   amendments to, 23–24
   and balance between states and
      federal government, 32, 33
   controversy over, 6
   as inspiration for other govern-
      ments, 6
   as oldest constitution currently in
      use, 6
   preamble to, 27
   ratification of, 19
   and Supreme Court, 53–54

V

Virginia Declaration of Rights, 23

W

Washington, George, 42, 46

ABOUT THE AUTHOR

Bridey Heing is a writer and book critic based in Washington, DC. She holds degrees in political science and international affairs from DePaul University and Washington University in Saint Louis. Her areas of focus are comparative politics and Iranian politics. Her master's thesis explores the evolution of populist politics and democracy in Iran since 1900. She has written about Iranian affairs, women's rights, and art and politics for publications like the *Economist*, Hyperallergic, and the Establishment. She also writes about literature and film. She enjoys traveling, reading, and exploring Washington's many museums.

PHOTO CREDITS